Trial or Triumph? Fact or Fiction of the Gifted

by Nancy Polette

Illustrated by John Steele

Pieces of Learning

CLC0425
ISBN 978-1-934358-07-8

2008 published by Pieces of Learning
Marion IL
Cover by John Steele

Dedication

For six gifted guys,

Daniel, Joshua, Sam, Tony, Avery, and Perrin

ACTORS AND ACTRESSES

Acting is all about honesty. If you can fake that, you've got it made.
George Burns (1896 - 1996)

Talk low, talk slow, and don't talk too much.
John Wayne (1907 - 1979)

Acting is not being emotional, but being able to express emotion.
Kate Reid (1930 - 1993)

The most difficult character in comedy is that of a fool, and he must be no simpleton who plays the part.
Miguel de Cervantes (1547 - 1616)

I love acting. It is so much more real than life.
Oscar Wilde (1854 - 1900)

Acting is merely the art of keeping a large group of people from coughing.
Sir Ralph Richardson (1902 - 1983)

Actors and Actresses

FACT OR FICTION?

After seeing her screen test,
officials at MGM refused to sign
Julie Andrews to a contract.

Julie Andrews

In 1947, Joe Pasternak, the Hollywood producer, was searching for a new child star. "Why not test that little Andrews girl that sings in the Hippodrome Revue?" a co-worker suggested. Twelve-year-old Julie was dressed up with ribbons and curls and brought to London's MGM Studios for a screen test.

When Joe Pasternak saw Julie he shook his head. He saw a child with bandy legs, buck teeth and heard a voice that could span four octaves and hit F above high C. Certainly this funny looking child with the freak voice did not have the makings of a child star. Julie failed the screen test.

Born in Surrey, England in 1935, Julie Andrews began singing lessons at the age of eight, when, strange as it may seem, she had a fully developed voice. Her mother was not the least discouraged with MGM's rejection. Voice lessons continued leading to radio and television spots. Soon Julie was traveling throughout Great Britain making Music Hall appearances. It was not long before her magnificent voice caught the public's attention. At age 13 she appeared in a command performance before the King and Queen of England.

Sadly, Julie's mother and stepfather were alcoholics. When Julie brought home more and more pay from her engagements, they stopped working, and Julie supported the family.

By the time she was 20 Julie starred in the musical The Boy Friend on both London and New York City stages. By now braces had taken care of the buck teeth and her legs were no longer spindly.

One success led to another. She starred in the Broadway musicals of My Fair Lady and Cinderella and won the Academy Award as best actress for her movie role as Mary Poppins.

If Joe Pasternak was there on award night, he most likely shook his head in disbelief. How could this beautiful, talented woman be that same "ugly duckling" he had tested years earlier and pronounced "unfilmable?" Joe's "ugly duckling" had, indeed become a swan.

FACT OR FICTION?

Doris Day's life reflected
her happy "girl next door"
screen image.

Doris Day

For more than 20 years Doris Day (born Doris von Kapelhoff in Cincinnati in 1924) was known to her fans as the sweet, lovable "girl next door" whose dazzling smile told the world there was no such thing as hard luck in life.

In real life Doris had more than her share of hard luck. Her parents divorced when she was ten. Her dream to become a dancer was shattered along with her right leg in an automobile accident at age 13. Getting to school on crutches was nearly impossible. She dropped out of school in her sophomore year. Just as the leg started to heal she took a bad fall and shattered the bone again. Doris spent nearly a year in a heavy cast.

Doris's mother was worried. Her busy, on-the-go daughter could not be allowed to do nothing for a year. Before her accident Doris often sang around the house. A friend suggested that her voice might have possibilities. Doris began singing lessons. The friend was right!

In her teens Doris began a career as a radio performer. The radio audience loved her mellow voice. Each listener felt she was singing directly to them. So did the composers, Jule Styne and Sammy Cahn who heard Doris sing at a party. In 1948, they signed her to do the movie Romance on the High Seas, and a major movie star was born! In the next 20 years Doris Day starred in 39 films. Perhaps now all the hard times were behind her.

But more trials were ahead.

In 1968, after years of making films and earning large salaries, Doris was shocked to find herself one half million dollars in debt. Her third husband had wiped out all of her earnings. There was no choice but to go back to work. For the next five years she starred in the Doris Day Show and numerous other television specials to pay off the enormous debt.

The "girl next door" with the sunny smile had more than her share of trials, but the strong woman underneath faced and overcame each one.

FACT OR FICTION?

After his first TV appearance,
Leonardo Di Caprio
was told never to come back.

Leonardo DiCaprio

Leonardo DiCaprio was born in Los Angeles, California, in 1974. Five years later he made his first television appearance as one of the children on the popular Romper Room show. His television career began and ended that same day. He yelled, he ran around, he disrupted the cast and crew, and no one could control him. He was told not to return the next day.

Raised by very easy-going but loving parents, Leonardo spent his childhood in what he calls the "ghetto" of Hollywood. It was a rough neighborhood. Just getting from one end of a block to another was a trial. Leonardo could easily have ended up in a gang with a criminal record, but his parents sent him to a school some distance away. Not only was he assured a good education, but his friends were boys from better neighborhoods.

His first acting job was a commercial for Matchbox Cars®. He was a popular choice for commercials aimed at children since he looked much younger than his actual age and could learn lines and follow directions more easily than a younger actor.

Leonardo moved from doing more than 30 commercials to being a cast member on various television shows and finally to movies. In The Quick and the Dead, This Boys' Life, and What's Eating Gilbert Grape he played a troubled teen. His big break came with his role as Jack Dawson in Titanic. Many fans saw the movie six or more times. "Leomania" broke out everywhere. The little boy who was sent home from Romper Room had truly become a star!

FACT OR FICTION?

Michael J. Fox
was a high school dropout

Michael J. Fox

Some fans know him as Marty McFly, others know him as Alex P. Keaton or Mike Flaherty, all television roles played by Michael J. Fox. Born in Alberta, Canada, in 1961, this five-foot- four actor set his sights on being a hockey star. As a ten-year-old he knew ice hockey was his game even though he acquired more than 50 stitches from injuries. In the next few years his teammates grew larger and larger. Michael was still short. Professional hockey was not a practical dream.

Michael turned to music and acting classes. At the same time a Canadian television show, Leo and Me, was looking for a twelve-year-old to play an important part. Michael at age 15 won the part. Even today he looks much younger than his actual age. He took other acting jobs that kept him busy both day and night. As a result, he missed so many days of high school that he dropped out.

At age 18 Michael headed for California but did not find the instant success he hoped for. He had minor parts in a few movies and television shows and then experienced a long dry spell of no acting jobs. He sold his car and some of his furniture to get money for food and thought seriously about going home.

The lucky break came with his audition for a part in Family Ties. He won the part and his career took off. Michael became one of the best known actors in Hollywood.

In 1991, Michael was filming the movie, Doc Hollywood, when he experienced weakness and stiffness in his left arm and twitching in his fingers. Medical tests revealed Parkinson's disease. For the next seven years he tried to keep his condition a secret but finally told his fans in an interview with Barbara Walters on 20/20.

Since his semi-retirement in 1999 Michael J. Fox has devoted his time to the Michael J. Fox Foundation for Parkinson's Research. Through speeches and a book about his life, more than 40 million dollars has been raised. In helping others, the small boy has become a very big man, indeed!

FACT OR FICTION?

Morgan J. Freeman
made his stage debut
as a dancer.

Morgan J. Freeman

The little boy was bored with school work. Recess was not fun either, since he didn't shine in athletics. But his ears perked up when there was talk of a school play. Eight-year-old Morgan Freeman tried out for a part and got the lead role. Schoolwork picked up after this! Four years later Morgan won a state-wide drama contest, and when high school days were over he was offered a drama scholarship to Jackson State University.

Morgan's passion for acting was matched by his passion for aircraft. He turned down the scholarship and entered the Air Force where he soon discovered that life as an Air Force mechanic was not nearly as exciting as the lives of the gallant flyers he saw in World War II movies. When his tour of duty was up he headed for Hollywood without a nickle in his pocket. Morgan was determined to make good as an actor.

Morgan worked as a clerk during the day and took classes in acting, singing and dancing at night. He proved to be a very good dancer and got his first stage job for pay as a dancer at the World's Fair in 1964. Morgan returned to New York and got his first big break in the TV series *The Electric Company*. For four years he had a steady paycheck playing the parts of Easy Reader, the Mad Scientist, and Count Dracula.

A series of small movie roles followed until, at the age of 50, Morgan Freeman was discovered! Roles in Driving Miss Daisy and The Shawshank Redemption established him as a major star. He was nominated for an Academy Award for Best Actor in Driving Miss Daisy and won the Academy Award for Best Supporting Actor in Million Dollar Baby.

Morgan Freeman, born in Memphis, Tennessee, in 1937, returned to his birth place more than 50 years later as a highly respected actor to donate a quarter million dollars to establish a Chair of Performing Arts at the Hutchison School for Girls. His life today is one that reaps the rewards of hard work without ever forgetting the hard times of the past.

FACT OR FICTION?

Judy Garland's studio bosses controlled everything she ate.

Judy Garland

Imagine the whole world knowing your name. Imagine earning thousands of dollars as a major movie star at age 16. Judy Garland (born Frances Gumm in 1922) could tell you what life would be like. Up at four in the morning for studio make-up; half a grapefruit for breakfast; learning lines between takes; taking time out each day to attend the MGM school; beef broth for lunch; working in front of the camera under hot lights for 8-12 hours a day; a very small dinner; more lines to learn for the next day; drop exhausted and hungry in bed after midnight; repeat day after day.

Judy Garland was such a hit in The Wizard of Oz that the studio kept her working non stop turning out film after film. To keep up the frantic pace and to keep her weight down the studio bosses watched everything she ate. She was kept on a strict diet and given pills for energy during the day and given more pills to help her sleep at night. Those same pills would follow her throughout her life.

Judy's appeal to movie audiences was her sweet face and her very unusual voice which could soar from low notes to high notes. The deep emotion in each song was felt by both the singer and her listeners. The bright, happy, girl-next-door role that she played in the many "Andy Hardy" movies did not give a clue to the real Judy who was worn out and hungry most of the time and thought of herself as plain and unappealing.

By 1959 Judy had been a star for more than 30 years. Doctors told her that she had a serious illness and would never sing again. Judy fooled everyone. Not only did she recover, but she went on to make recordings, sing at Carnegie Hall, and star in her own television series.

Judy Garland brought much joy and happiness to movie goers all over the world. Her gift was more than her voice. It was the ability to find hope and happiness in every song she sang. How sad it was that she did not find hope and happiness in real life.

FACT OR FICTION?

Tom Hanks was voted
Mr. Popularity
by his high school class.

Tom Hanks

Far from being Mr. Popularity, Tom Hanks describes himself a a "geek" in high school. He says, "I was horribly, painfully, terribly shy. At the same time I was the guy who'd yell out funny captions during filmstrips." Tom was named "Class Clown" in his high school year book.

Tom Hanks was born in Concord, California, in 1956. When he was five years old his parents divorced, and Tom went to live with his father who moved around a lot. By the time Tom was ten he had attended five different schools and lived in ten different houses. It is hard to say whether Tom Hanks was a naturally shy kid or whether he avoided making friends because he knew the friendships couldn't last.

It was in high school that Tom found an outlet for his talent to clown. Parts in high school plays convinced Tom that acting was for him. After high school he studied theatre at Chabot College and Sacramento State University.

In 1979, Tom arrived in New York City and got a part in the television show Bosom Buddies. Director Ron Howard saw Tom in the show and signed him to do the movie Splash. Splash was a hit but unfortunately was followed by four flops. Tom's career continued like a roller coaster. He would make one fairly successful movie followed by more flops. Finally, in the 1990s he had a series of excellent films including A League of Their Own, Sleepless in Seattle, and Philadelphia for which he won the Academy Award for best actor.

Success meant that the public wanted to know more and more about Tom Hanks. Reporters discovered that the actor was a very down-to-earth person but was also a very private person. He was always willing to talk about his work but not about his private life. Today Tom Hanks continues acting and directing. He is a great supporter of NASA and of the World War II Memorial. He devotes time and energy to both.

FACT OR FICTION?

Bob Hope got his start
as a boxer
using the name Packy East.

Bob Hope

On March 30, 1908, William and Avis Hope herded their sons off the ship to set foot on Ellis Island, the staging point for all immigrants. Avis kept a special eye out for five-year-old Leslie Hope who was the cut-up of the family. They entered New York City with little money but high expectations.

The Hope sons found whatever work they could. Leslie, who would later change his name to Bob, thought he could earn big money as a boxer. He took the name, Packy East, lost his first few bouts, and decided singing and dancing along the local board walk was an easier way to earn money. Bob's funny patter made him a natural as a song and dance comedian in vaudeville. When he was 25, his act caught the attention of another famous comedian who arranged for Bob and his dancing partner to have a screen test. Bob, who was always sure of himself, had his confidence shaken when they failed the screen test.

Never discouraged for long, Bob found parts in Broadway musicals and made his way to Hollywood in the mid 1930s. After small parts in a few movies, he was a hit in the film Big Broadcast of 1938. After this success Bob's career was off and running.

He made films. He toured the country with a live stage show. His weekly radio show was one of the most popular on the air. Later, he took his talents to television for a total of 64 years of broadcasting.

Bob Hope always had a warm place in his heart and great respect for those who serve their country in the armed forces. His first tour to entertain the troops was in 1941. Where the troops went, Bob Hope went...through World War II, the Korean War, the Vietnam War, and the Persian Gulf War (this last tour when he was 85 years old!) In a 50-year period he made 60 tours all over the world to entertain the troops. Imagine what the troops would have missed if he had decided to stay a boxer or had given up performing after that first failed screen test!

Bob Hope at 100 years old was living proof it is possible to go from trial to triumph.

FACT OR FICTION?

Christopher Reeve,
known for his role as Superman,
had a fear of flying.

Christopher Reeve

Far from having a fear of flying, Christopher Reeve piloted his own plane solo across the Atlantic Ocean twice. In addition he was an expert ice hockey player, sailor, scuba diver, skier, and horseman. He composed and played classical music, starred in 17 feature films, 12 television movies and 150 plays. No challenge seemed too great for this talented actor who not only played the part of Superman but seemed to *be* a superman!

Christopher Reeve (born in 1952 in New York City) began his acting career at the age of 15 with the Williamstown Theatre Festival in Massachusetts. After high school and university days he worked as an apprentice at London's Old Vic Theatre. Part of his work there was teaching British actors to speak with an American accent. He skipped his last university year to accept a place at the Juilliard School of Performing Arts. This was followed by parts in stage plays and in the soap opera Love of Life.

Chris's big break came in 1978, when he was chosen to play the lead in the movie Superman. The movie was a huge success and allowed Chris to choose future movie roles.

In 1995, at the age of 43, Christopher Reeve was to face the greatest challenge of his life. His horse, Eastern Express, stopped suddenly before a rail jump and Reeve was pitched forward and landed on his head and broke his neck. For the rest of his life Christopher Reeve was confined to a wheel chair, unable to move, and completely dependent on others.

Expert medical care stabilized his injuries but could not reverse the paralysis. Despite the terrible injuries, Christopher Reeve appeared one year later to speak at the Academy Awards and to host the Paralympics games in Atlanta. As chairman of the American Paralysis Association he fought for increased funding for spinal cord research and higher insurance coverage for those who had sustained such injuries. No challenge was too great for this "superman." He raised more than 55 million dollars for research in the nine years before his death in 2004.

FACT OR FICTION?

Universal Studios signed Elizabeth Taylor
to a lifetime contract
after her first movie.

Elizabeth Taylor

Elizabeth Taylor was nine years old when she made her first and last movie for Universal Studios. The casting director thought "her eyes were too old and she would never make it as a child star." After that first movie she was fired.

Elizabeth's mother, her greatest fan, took her to MGM Studios where she rose to stardom with her second film National Velvet. Elizabeth, born in England in 1932, found that life as a child star was not easy. The strict teacher at the MGM School demanded lots of homework. The movie director expected Elizabeth to memorize her lines perfectly. She was pulled from make up, to costumes, to lighting, to publicity photographs in between movie takes. At home it was not unusual for the little girl to feel the blows of an alcoholic father even though she was the sole support of the family.

As a teen, life for Elizabeth was school and work. There was no time for dates, proms, or basketball games. Boys were afraid to ask her out, and in groups of young people her age she was shy and quiet.

Unlike many other child actors, Elizabeth made the transition from child to adult star easily. She won the Academy Award for Butterfield 8, the first of many awards that recognized her as a gifted actress. Unfortunately, the little girl who never felt truly loved, was married eight times. Each time she felt she had found the love she was seeking, and each time she was wrong.

In her later years, despite having suffered a broken back, a brain tumor, pneumonia, and heart failure, Elizabeth Taylor works tirelessly for the Foundation she helped to start, raising millions of dollars for research on AIDS. A great lady and a great star, she is known as a steadfast friend but above all, after fifty years of stardom, she is a survivor!

FACT OR FICTION?

John Wayne got his start in films
as a singing cowboy.

John Wayne

His name was "Singin Sandy." He was dressed all in white from cowboy hat to boots, and he crooned tender western ballads into the camera. This was John Wayne in the early 1930s' westerns. Of course he could neither sing nor play the guitar, so a guitarist and singer stood out of camera range to supply the sound while "Duke" mouthed the words.

John Wayne (Marion Morrison) was born in Iowa in 1907. When he was six years old his family tried homesteading in rural California. Living on the edge of the Mojave desert with no electricity or running water, the family kept up a running battle with snakes and rodents. When the family finally moved into town, Marion had other fights to win. He was constantly teased about his name. When one friend called him "Duke" (which was his dog's name) the name stuck and the teasing stopped.

It didn't take long for his classmates to discover that he was an excellent student and a powerhouse on the football field. Fox Studios hired local football players to move furniture and scenery. Director, John Ford, watched the strong, good looking "Duke" easily move heavy scenery and gave him a part in a submarine picture. Soon after, he was given the screen name John Wayne. He would make more than 200 films over a 50- year period.

Since no one is perfect, especially movie stars, John Wayne did have his odd moments. He was highly superstitious. He would never allow a hat to be placed on a bed. That meant someone would be out of work. An umbrella opened in the house would bring bad luck. Accepting a salt shaker from another's hand meant bad luck. The shaker had to be set down on the table first.

While he was not particularly fond of horses, John Wayne did take to adventure and the outdoors. He was strong enough to win a battle over cancer in 1964. He recovered and made 18 more movies in the next fourteen years.

FACT OR FICTION?

Guards surrounded Kate Winslett
who wore the $3.5 million replica of the Titanic jewel
at the Academy Awards.

Kate Winslett

It was not Kate Winslett who wore the 3.5 million dollar Titanic jewel, but the much slimmer Celine Dion, who sang the title song for the movie. Did the jewelers think the Heart of the Ocean sapphire and diamond necklace would look better on Celine? No one knows for sure.

Kate Winsett's weight has often been a trial for others but not for her. As a teenager she made serious efforts to lose weight and might have injured her health if she had continued. Kate wisely decided that her weight was not a problem for her and others could accept her as she was.

This talented actress (born in England in 1975) has earned four Oscar nominations and five Golden Globe nominations for demanding roles in which she suffered poverty, heartbreak, a prison sentence for murder, a near drowning experience, loss of memory, and a host of other roles for which movie critics had only praise. By age 21, she received two Oscar nominations and by age 30, four nominations.

It would have been unusual for Kate to become anything but an actress. Both her parents and grandparents were actors as well as both of her sisters. She began acting lessons at the Redroofs Theatre School when she was 11. One year later she made her first television commercial for a cereal, and at age 15 she was acting in a BBC television series.

Kate landed her first film role as a co-star in 1994 with Heavenly Creatures. The critics loved her and her film career took off with Sense and Sensibility and in 1997, Titanic, which earned more than one billion dollars at the box office.

With so many nominations for the top movie awards and so many favorable reviews by film critics, it is only a matter of time before Kate Winslett wins a top award. For Kate, her weight is not a trial – her acting is the triumph!

ATHLETES

Small opportunities
are often the beginning
of great enterprises.
Demosthenes

You have to
recognize when the
right place and the right
time fuse and take advantage of that opportunity. There are
plenty of opportunities out there. You can't sit back and wait.
Ellen Metcalf

Sports serve society by providing vivid examples of excellence.
George W. Will

Sports do not build character, they reveal it.
Heywood Braun

It's not so important who starts the game but who finishes it.
John Wooden

Desire is the most important factor in the success
of any athlete.
Willie Shoemaker

For when the One Great Scorer comes
To write against your
name,
He marks - not
that you won
or lost -
But how you played
the game.
Grantland Rice

Athletes

FACT OR FICTION?

Two broken ankles
were both good and bad luck
for Hank Aaron.

Hank Aaron

It was a hot summer day in 1951 when a stranger stood watching a softball game. The players were teen-agers, and one player in particular stood out as a cross-handed hitter. Hank Aaron was the hitter, and Ed Scott, a scout for the Mobile Bears, was the stranger. Ed Scott asked seven-teen-year-old Hank to play with the Bears.

Later in the season when the Bears played the Indianapolis Clowns, the Clowns signed Hank to a contract paying $200 a month. In 1952 this was a big salary.

At age eighteen Hank left Alabama for Indiana. He left his parents and seven brothers and sisters. He left a house with no bathroom and no elec-tricity. The low pay his father made working in a shipyard was barely enough to feed the family. Nevertheless there were many times to come when he would miss his home and family.

Hank's time with the Clowns was short. A scout for the Milwaukee Braves saw Hank play, recognized the boy's gifts as a player, and signed him up. Hank was to play in the minor leagues until the coaches thought he was ready. It was then that a broken ankle gave Hank his big chance.

Bobby Thompson. the Braves' left fielder, broke an ankle during spring training. Hank Aaron was chosen to be his replacement for the 1954 sea-son. Before the season ended, Hank broke an ankle sliding into third base. It was a good luck, bad luck year. He would not play again until the next season.

By 1956, Hank Aaron had become the National League batting cham-pion. Hank seemed so relaxed at the plate that some pitchers thought he was asleep. They quickly found out he was not. In 1974, at the age of forty, Hank Aaron broke Babe Ruth's home run record of 714 . He would go on to achieve a total of 755 home runs.

In 1951, Hank Aaron's parents would never have guessed that in 1975 the whole world would be cheering for their son. Hank broke records not through luck but through skill, hard work, and determination.

FACT OR FICTION?

Lance Armstrong
won his first gold medal
in the 1992 Olympics.

Lance Armstrong

From a very early age Lance Armstrong showed he had "staying power." He was not the strongest athlete or the fastest runner in school, but he could remain in a race, whether cycling, swimming, or running longer than most other athletes.

Because of his stamina Lance won the Iron Kids Triathlon at age thirteen. The race required swimming, cycling, and running. Lance knew that he was best at cycling and joined a cycling team which won a seven-day race. After that win, he was sure he was ready for the 1992 Summer Olympics expecting to win a medal. Not only was there no medal, but he came in fourteenth in the race. In his first professional race after that he came in last. But Lance was not a quitter.

Hard work paid off. One year later in 1993, he won the World Championship Road Race. Victory followed victory until in 1993, he learned he had cancer that had spread throughout his body. He was given a short time to live.

Lance battled the cancer the same way he trained for races. He had many painful treatments. For three months he became weaker, and weaker but his strength returned in l997. Not only had he beaten the cancer, but he went into training for the next race.

He trained in Texas. He trained in Europe. He found the toughest terrains and highest hills. After his long illness, people admired Lance Armstrong for entering the tough 1999 Tour de France race. No one expected him to win. He not only won the race, but he repeated his win each year for the next six years.

Today Lance Armstrong applies the same determination used in winning races to helping others in the fight against cancer. The Lance Armstrong Foundation has raised tens of millions of dollars toward research that may one day find a way to prevent the disease.

FACT OR FICTION?

After being drafted in 1942,
Jackie Robinson became the star
of the Army baseball team.

Jackie Robinson

In 1943, when Jackie Robinson was drafted into the United States Army, he could easily have been the star of the Army baseball team. The problem as the Army saw it was that he would have to play on an all black team, and there was no black team.

Born in Georgia in 1919, Jackie and his family moved to Pasadena, California, a year later. As small as he was he showed a talent for baseball at an early age. Jackie's mother supported the family by cleaning houses, and when he was old enough, Jackie helped out by doing yard work and delivering papers.

Jackie's mother was determined that her children should have an education. In high school Jackie showed talent in every sport he tried. At Pasadena Junior College he starred in both football and baseball and won a scholarship to UCLA.

After his time in the Army, Jackie did not return to college. In 1946 he was playing baseball with an all Negro team when he was offered a place with the Brooklyn Dodgers by its President Branch Rickey.

After a time with the Dodger's farm club in Montreal, Jackie played his first game for the Dodgers in April of 1947. Some of his teammates gave him a hard time. Many Dodger fans yelled hateful words at him. As the first black player in the Major Leagues, Jackie accepted the slights with dignity. Two years later he had the full support of his team and was named the most valuable player in the National League.

Not only did Jackie Robinson open the door to baseball for other black players, he continued to fight for Civil Rights. He retired from baseball in 1957, and in 1962, was elected to the Baseball Hall of Fame . . . an exceptional player and a true gentleman.

FACT OR FICTION?

Nolan Ryan could pitch a baseball at a speed of 105 miles per hour.

Nolan Ryan

He was six feet two inches tall, slender, and soft spoken. He didn't talk much and was polite to everyone he met. With his 105 miles per hour pitch he was the most feared pitcher in all of baseball. His nickname was "The Ryan Express."

Nolan Ryan , a baseball legend, was born in 1947, in a small town in Texas. Growing up with no television or video games, the six Ryan children spent a lot of time in outdoor games. From a very early age Nolan liked throwing things. If he didn't have a ball he would go down to the Bayou and throw rocks at snakes and frogs. Baseball games took place on a nearby vacant lot, and Nolan played on Little League teams from the age of nine.

A scout for the New York Mets watched Nolan play for his high school team and recognized the boy's gift as a fast ball pitcher. Two years later in 1965, Nolan signed with the Mets but did not find immediate success as a pitcher. There was no doubt he had a fast pitch, but he could not control it. More than one batter suffered a broken helmet, or worse yet, a broken arm. Nolan's pitches were wild, and it was evident that speed was not enough.

In 1971, the Mets traded Nolan to the California Angels. With help from team members and the pitching coach, Nolan began to get control of the ball. Day after day he threw pitches. Over and over he practiced getting the ball exactly where he wanted it. He pitched despite injuries to his elbow, ankle, and back.

The boy who showed promise as a ball player in high school could have given up his dream to be a professional player many times. His gift of speed could only be realized by gaining control over the ball. He practiced eight to nine hours a day, every day of each seven-month season. By 1973, he pitched two no hitters and had his first 20 win season. By the time of his retirement in 1993, Nolan Ryan had played for 27 years with 5,714 strikeouts and 52 major league records.

GOVERNMENT AND LAW

***The first duty of a leader is to make himself be loved without courting love. To be loved without 'playing up' to anyone - even to himself.* Andre Malraux**

A sense of humor is part of the art of leadership, of getting along with people, of getting things done.
Dwight D. Eisenhower

The crowd gives the leader new strength.
Evenius

Faith in the ability of a leader is of slight service unless it be united with faith in his justice.
George Goethals

Leadership and learning are indispensable to each other.
John F. Kennedy

After two years in Washington, I often long for the realism and sincerity of Hollywood.
Fred Thompson

You know what's interesting about Washington? It's the kind of place where second-guessing has become second nature.
George W. Bush

The mystery of government is not how Washington works but how to make it stop.
P. J. O'Rourke

***I don't make jokes. I just watch the government and report the facts.* Will Rogers**

Government and Law

FACT OR FICTION?

Madeleine Albright
kept three men in her office
at all times.

Madeleine Albright

If there had been gifted programs when Madeleine Albright went to school she would have been one of the first selected. This very bright and dedicated woman took office as the first woman Secretary of State forty years after she became a United States citizen. One of the first things she did in her new office in 1997 was to hang portraits of three men. These men symbolized for her the precious freedom she and her family found in the United States. One was Thomas Jefferson, the first secretary of state. The second was Edmund Muskie, her former boss, and the third was General George C. Marshall who led the recovery of Europe after World War II.

Madeleine's family had to flee Czechoslovakia in 1939, when the country was invaded by the German army. Madeleine's grandparents were not so fortunate and were sent to concentration camps. The family spent the war years in London and returned to Czechoslovakia after the war where Madeleine's father served as a Czech diplomat. When the Communists seized power in 1948, the family had to flee once again, this time to the United States. Nine years later Madeleine became a U.S. citizen.

After her marriage to Joseph Albright and becoming the mother of three daughters, Madeleine earned her Ph.D. in Public Law and Government. She worked hard at her studies and found that learning languages was easy. When she met with Russian leaders as Secretary of State, they were surprised that she could easily speak their language.

Before becoming Secretary of State Madeleine Albright served in many government posts including that of United States Ambassador to the United Nations. She brought not only her knowledge to every job she undertook but worked hard to bring about international cooperation and understanding among the countries of the world. She had learned first hand as a child how precious freedom and democracy were.

FACT OR FICTION?

Hillary Rodham Clinton
graduated last
in her college class.

Hillary Rodham Clinton

Hillary Clinton, former First Lady of the United States, would have been accepted into any gifted program in any school she attended. Earning high grades and honors throughout her academic career, she was Valedictorian of her college graduating class.

She earned her law degree from Yale where she met Bill Clinton. She saw him in the Yale Library, thought he was a nice looking fellow, and introduced herself. They were married five years later. She gave Bill her full support when he ran for Governor of Arkansas, and it was during her time as First Lady of Arkansas that their daughter, Chelsea, was born.

When Bill ran for president Hillary campaigned with him. She toured the country and met with thousands of people. At the same time, daughter Chelsea was never forgotten. Hillary would stop on the campaign trail every few days to go home and spend time with Chelsea. If Chelsea thought she could skip her homework while her mother was traveling, she was wrong. She had to FAX her homework to Hillary for checking.

As First Lady of the United States Hillary took on the job of developing a health plan for all Americans. She traveled the country to find out from the people and from health care providers what was needed. While Congress turned down the plan, it was the first step in trying to solve a big problem. Hillary has often been criticized for being too strong, too intelligent, and too outspoken.

When the Clintons left the White House it was these qualities that got her elected as the first woman senator from New York. Only the voters will one day decide if she becomes the first woman president of the United States.

FACT OR FICTION?

Sandra Day O'Connor
turned down 30 job offers
after graduating third in her law school class.

Sandra Day O'Connor

Sandra Day O'Connor, the first female Associate Justice of the United Sates Supreme Court, received no job offers after graduating from law school despite the fact that she ranked third in her class.

Justice O'Connor (born in 1930 in El Paso, Texas) grew up on a cattle ranch in Texas. For the first eight years of her life she was an only child. She read at the age of four, drove a tractor, and learned to shoot by the age of ten. Some said she could hit a coyote between the eyes at 40 paces. Sandra's parents were worried that the small school house available to ranch children would not give their daughter the education she needed. When Sandra was six years old, they sent her to live with her grandparents in El Paso where she could have better schooling.

Sandra excelled at her studies whether at Austin High School in El Paso or Stanford University in California. Since no one wanted to hire a woman lawyer, Sandra got a job as a law clerk after graduation. Marriage and children and a move to Arizona followed, and knowing no law firm would hire a young mother, Sandra opened her own law firm. The task of balancing motherhood with full time work as a lawyer proved difficult. She took five years off to be a full time mom but stayed active in local politics.

In 1965, Sandra went to work part time as assistant attorney-general for the State of Arizona. She moved quickly to become attorney general, a member of the state legislature, and the Arizona State Majority Leader. In 1974, she won election as a judge for the Maricopa County Superior Court and later moved to the Arizona Court of Appeals.

In 1981, Sandra Day O'Connor was appointed to the Supreme Court of the United States. Seven years later she was diagnosed with cancer. Friends urged her to retire, but she knew there was work still to be done. She remained at her post during her treatment and overcame the illness. She continued to serve with distinction for another eight years.

Sandra Day O'Connor exemplifies the philosophy she lives by. Any trial can be overcome with determination. Triumph will follow!

FACT OR FICTION?

At P.S. 39 Colin Powell
was placed in a class
for slow learners.

Colin Powell

Born in New York City in 1937, Colin Powell was introduced to war at a very early age. The United States entered World War II in December of 1941. When Colin and his friends weren't shooting down imaginary enemy planes with imaginary weapons, they attended Public School #39 where Colin was placed in a class for slow learners.

Throughout his elementary and high school years Colin Powell was not an academic star. It wasn't until he attended City College in 1954, that he discovered the ROTC. The military education was exactly what he was looking for. He excelled in his military classes and became a leader in the elite group the Pershing Rifles.

Upon graduation from college, Colin Powell entered the Army as a second lieutenant. He continued to take the toughest assignments the Army had to offer including tours of Vietnam. It was in Vietnam in 1969, that Colin Powell became a hero.

The helicopter in which he was riding crashed, and Powell, despite a broken ankle and surrounding flames, pulled several men to safety. For this act he received the Soldier's Medal for bravery.

For the next thirty years Colin Power would lead troops in Vietnam, Germany, and South Korea; as commander of Desert Storm; as head of the Joint Chiefs of Staff, and finally as Secretary of State of the United States.

While Powell was trained as a fighting man, he believed that going to war was a last resort when nations disagreed. As Secretary of State he worked as diligently for peace as he had as a leader of men in war time.

FACT OR FICTION?

Condoleezza Rice
gave her first piano concert
at the age of four.

Condoleezza Rice

Condoleezza Rice was born in Birmingham, Alabama, in 1954, the daughter of a minister and a school teacher. Condoleezza's mother was a gifted pianist and began giving Condoleezza piano lessons at the age of three. The little girl showed a talent for the piano and gave her first recital when she was four years old. For a time she thought she might become a concert pianist, but in her teen years she knew that being a very good pianist wasn't good enough.

Condoleezza excelled at nearly every task she undertook. In school she skipped both the first and seventh grades. She was an avid reader, and at age fifteen she took college courses while in high school. It was inevitable that during these growing up years that she should suffer discrimination. Her elementary school was for black students only. There were only certain restaurants and hotels where black people could eat and sleep. There were even separate drinking fountains for blacks and whites. Condoleezza knew that education was the key to abolishing discrimination.

It was at the University of Denver that she discovered her passion for foreign relations. She graduated with honors at age nineteen and went on to Notre Dame University for a Masters Degree and back to the University of Denver for her Ph.D. She accepted a job as Professor of Political Science at Stanford University.

President George H. Bush heard about Condoleezza's extraordinary knowledge of foreign affairs, and she was asked to come to Washington as an advisor. After a time she returned to Stanford and served as Provost for six years. She thought her Washington days were over.

This was not to be. When George W. Bush ran for president he wanted Condoleezza's help with foreign policy. When he was elected, he appointed her National Security Advisor, the first woman to hold that job.

In January of 2005, Condoleezza Rice became the Secretary of State of the United States. In this new position she would develop positive relations with countries around the world to "maintain security, fight poverty, and make democratic reforms." The little girl who could read music before words had become a world voice to be reckoned with!

SINGERS & MUSICIANS

"Art is the only thing you cannot punch a button for. You must do it the old-fashioned way. Stay up and really burn the midnight oil. There are no compromises.
Leontyne Price

After silence, that which comes nearest to expressing the inexpressible is music.
Aldous Huxley

I don't know anything about music. In my line you don't have to.
Elvis Presley

I think I should have no other mortal wants, if I could always have plenty of music. It seems to infuse strength into my limbs and ideas into my brain. Life seems to go on without effort, when I am filled with music.
George Eliot

There is no feeling, except the extremes of fear and grief, that does not find relief in music.
George Eliot

Among all men on the earth bards have a share of honor and reverence, because the muse has taught them songs and loves the race of bards.
Homer

Ah, music. A magic beyond all we do here!
J.K. Rowling,

Music is the only language in which you cannot say a mean or sarcastic thing.
John Erskine

Singers and Musicians

FACT OR FICTION?

Gloria Estevan's career
came to an end
after she suffered a severe injury.

Gloria Estevan

In 1990, Gloria Estevan was one of the world's most popular singers and song writers. Her blend of Latin and American music had universal appeal. A year earlier, her best selling album, *Cuts Both Ways*, sold ten million copies and was the best selling album in the United States, Great Britain, Holland, Belgium, Australia, and Japan. The little girl who fled Cuba with her family in 1959, had become the "Queen of Latin Pop."

It was also in March of 1990, that Gloria's life would see drastic change. She was resting in her tour bus as it made its way through Pennsylvania to perform a concert in New York. A tractor trailer hit the back of the tour bus, and Gloria was severely injured. Paramedics rushed to the scene and lifted her out of the bus window. When doctors at the closest hospital examined her the news was not good. Her back was broken. It was unlikely that she would ever walk again.

Gloria was taken by helicopter to New York City where surgeons implanted metal rods in her back. Months of painful physical therapy followed. Gloria was determined to do whatever it took to get back on her feet. And she did!

One year later Gloria Estevan appeared at the American Music Awards, produced another best selling album, and went on a tour that covered 100 cities. Not only was she singing and walking, but she was dancing as well.

Gloria Estevan never forgot her Hispanic heritage. She recorded in Spanish as well as English. She is proud of the fact that neither she nor her band do drugs or alcohol. In 1992, just two years after her accident, Gloria and her band raised two million dollars to help Miami victims of Hurricane Andrew.

Despite all the honors she has received, Gloria considers it the greatest compliment that she and her husband, Emilio, are considered by their friends and neighbors as "just plain folks." She takes great pride in her Latin roots and in knowing she can make a difference in the lives of those who need a helping hand.

FACT OR FICTION?

Ella Fitzgerald
got her start in show business
as a dancer.

Ella Fitzgerald

Ella Fitzgerald was born in Newport News, Virginia, in 1918. Within a short time she lost both of her parents and was placed in an orphanage where she spent all of her childhood. The little girl was a favorite in the orphanage because of her sunny disposition. She danced her way to meals and to classes, and when she was fifteen she entered an amateur contest determined to win as a dancer.

The place was New York's Apollo Theatre. As Ella made her way on stage, her knees shook so hard she could not dance. She began to sing songs she had learned from her mother. To her surprise she won the $25.00 prize, not for dancing but for singing!.

In the audience that night was a member of Chick Webb's famous band. He told Chick about the young girl with perfect pitch. Chick decided to give Ella a chance. His band was playing at Yale University the next night. Ella would sing with the band. If Yale liked her he would hire her. Ella sang her heart out. Yale students loved her. Chick hired Ella to sing with his band and took her home to his wife. Eventually the couple adopted her. Ella traveled with the band until Chick's death and continued to travel for another three years. Her voice ranged from D to high C. She could sing almost any type of music from swing to jazz. She became best known for her "scat" singing, making her voice sound like one of the instruments in the orchestra. Many called her a musician as well as a singer.

During her career Ella Fitzgerald earned the title "The First Lady of Song." She recorded seventy albums and more than two thousand songs. Duke Ellington and Cole Porter wrote songs for her. Her performances took her all over the world as her natural cheerfulness became part of her jazz interpretations.

In 1986 Ella became ill and had open heart surgery. Fans thought she would retire. One year later she returned to the stage, wowing fans with a voice as strong as ever. The "First Lady of Song" continued to entertain audiences until her death in 1996.

FACT OR FICTION?

Loretta Lynn wore long hair
when she performed
to hide the holes in her head.

Loretta Lynn

Growing up in Butcher Holler in the Depression years was a struggle for survival. The mountain folk were isolated from the rest of the world. There were no cars, electric lights, or refrigerators, and only two meals a day. Nothing was ever wasted. Chicken feet were used to make dumplings. Hog entrails were used to make lye soap. When Loretta Lynn was born her father had to sell the family milk cow to pay the old woman who took care of her mother.

Loretta as a toddler suffered severe ear infections. Her mother walked ten miles to the hospital day after day so the doctors could drill holes in Loretta's head to clear the infection. Loretta wore long hair when she performed to cover the scars.

Loretta was married at an early age and had four children by the time she was eighteen. About that time her husband Doolittle bought her a guitar. She taught herself to play and began composing songs about life in Butcher Holler. Doolittle got Loretta her first singing job at the Grange Hall for five dollars a night. Before long Loretta had her own group of musicians called "Loretta's Trail Blazers." Soon Loretta made her first record, and she and Doolittle traveled the country, stopping at every small radio station along the way to ask disk jockeys to play the record.

In 1960, Loretta had a chance to appear on "Grand Old Opry." Her career took off. She was invited back week after week and began recording for Decca Records and setting off on country-wide tours. Loretta was singing two hundred nights a year.

The coal miner's daughter had hit the Big Time! Loretta Lynn's gift of song made her the first woman named Entertainer of the Year and the first woman in country music to win a gold record. Throughout her life Loretta stayed true to her roots. Her songs tell of the people and the feelings she grew up with and help build a bridge between those who grew up poor and those fortunate enough to have three meals a day.

FACT OR FICTION?

Jim Nabors was hired
for the *Andy Griffith Show*
because of his rich singing voice.

Jim Nabors

Jim Nabors was born singing, yet his greatest fame came from playing the part of the lovable, but not too bright Gomer Pyle. He played the part first on the Andy Griffith Show and later on his own television series Gomer Pyle, U.S.M.C.

Jim Nabors was born in Slyacauga, Alabama, in 1930. He sang almost as soon as he could talk. From an early age it was evident that he had a gifted voice. He sang in the local church choir. He sang in his high school glee club. As a young man he sang in local clubs at night while working as an NBC film cutter during the day.

One night in 1962, Jim was performing at a Santa Monica club. In the audience was Andy Griffith, star of the popular Andy Griffith Show. Andy was not nearly as impressed with Jim's rich baritone voice as he was with Jim's remarks between songs. He asked Jim to audition for the show and Jim became known to millions as a cheerful hick with the high voice named Gomer Pyle.

Jim enjoyed his fame on the Andy Griffith Show as well as playing Gomer for five years on his own show but still wanted to achieve notice as a singer. Carol Burnett insisted that Jim brought her luck on the Carol Burnett Show by appearing in the opening show of every season.

In the 1960s and 70s Jim recorded dozens of albums. Several were successful, but his music appealed more to older generations than to rock and roll fans. His rich almost operatic voice was not suited to rock or pop music. He was a popular Las Vegas performer for many years.

He retired to Hawaii after a serious illness that made a liver transplant necessary. He enjoys life today on the macadamia nut farm that he owns. A highway near his home town is named the Jim Nabors Highway.

Jim will always be fondly remembered as Gomer Pyle. the recruit who never made it out of boot camp. The Marines, however, had other ideas. In 2001 Jim donned his Marine Corps uniform to take part in a ceremony that promoted him to the rank of Lance Corporal. He wears his new stripes with pride!

TELEVISION ACTORS AND PERSONALITIES

Television is more interesting than people. If it were not, we would have people standing in the corners of our rooms.
Alan Corenk

Television has proved that people will look at anything rather than each other.
Ann Landers

Television is the first truly democratic culture - the first culture available to everybody and entirely governed by what the people want. The most terrifying thing is what people do want.
Clive Barnes

The one function TV news performs very well is that when there is no news we give it to you with the same emphasis as if there were.
David Brinkley

TV is chewing gum for the eyes.
Frank Lloyd Wright

Television news is like a lightning flash. It makes a loud noise, lights up everything around it, leaves everything else in darkness and then is suddenly gone.
Hodding Carter

Television is for appearing on - not for looking at. *Noel Coward*

Television Actors and Personalities

FACT OR FICTION?

Alan Alda, "Hawkeye" in MASH, was a real gunnery officer in Korea.

Alan Alda

Alfonso D'Abruzzo (Alan Alda) was practically born on a stage. His father, who later became a well-known actor, traveled the vaudeville circuit performing in one city after another. Alan and his mother traveled with him, and the young boy spent many hours back stage in a variety of theatres.

When Alan was seven the travels ceased. He was stricken with polio. For two years his parents worked tirelessly with him, applying hot towels and massaging his legs, helping him to walk again.

After the boy's recovery, his father was offered leading roles in Hollywood, and the family moved to California. Alan had his first taste of school there (he had been taught by tutors) and quickly discovered that school bullies cannot be put off with acting and jokes.

Alan knew from an early age that he wanted to be an actor. After getting a university degree he studied acting in Europe for a year. He then joined the U.S. Army Reserve and spent six months in Korea as a gunnery officer.

With his acting skills, combined with his knowledge of Korea, Alan was well prepared for his role as Hawkeye Pierce in the long running television series MASH. The series also gave him a chance to write and direct. He wrote thirteen of the episodes and helped in writing many others. He directed twenty. MASH ran for eleven years, and during that time Alan Alda was nominated for 21 Emmy Awards. He was the first person to win an Emmy Award for writing, acting, and directing the same series.

When MASH ended its run Alda appeared on stage and in motion pictures in a variety of roles. He returned to television in 2004 as a senator in the popular West Wing. He has always been a strong supporter of women's rights and considered running for the U.S. Senate in 1995 but decided his talents lay elsewhere.

Alan Alda overcame polio, a fractured education, a difficult family life, and many tough years as a struggling young actor before achieving success. His success is due to hard work and the philosophy he lives by, "Change what you can but accept those things that cannot be changed."

FACT OR FICTION?

Carol Burnett pretended to be her own twin sister.

Carol Burnett

Imagine a little girl being told by her mother that she should be a writer. That way no one would have to look at her. Imagine the same little girl living with parents who cared more for alcohol than their daughter.

Carol Burnett was born in San Antonio, Texas, in 1933. As a young child she showed a talent for mimicking others. Her mother frequently gave her a slap across the face for crossing her eyes and making funny faces. Fortunately Carol Burnett had a wise grandmother who took her away from her parents and raised her in a boarding house in Hollywood, California. Throughout their lives Carol and her grandmother had a loving relationship.

At the boarding house the nine-year-old fooled the other residents by pretending to be her own twin sister. She would appear in the parlor in one outfit and a few minutes later change clothes and appear again. She would enter the front door and greet everyone, and then in the wink of an eye, take the fire escape and come down the stairs. It was a great game, but after a time proved too hard to keep up.

After high school Carol enrolled at the University of California and managed to get a few bit parts on TV shows. It was 1959, when Carol got her big break. She appeared on Broadway in the musical Once Upon A Mattress and became a regular on the popular Garry Moore Show. This eventually led to Carol getting her own variety show. TV executives gave her one year to make the show a success. The show ran for more than ten years.

The lady who was best known for her Tarzan yell and for pulling her ear at the end of each show, brought laughter to millions. When the Carol Burnett Show ended she appeared in several movies and as a guest star on other television series. She is a strong spokesperson against drug abuse, holds strong opinions about honest journalism, and never hesitates to give an autograph and to stop and talk with fans. Carol Burnett is thankful for the life her talent has given her and never fails to remember her modest beginnings.

FACT OR FICTION?

Andy Griffith was a high school English teacher.

Andy Griffith

As a young man, Andy Griffith had a hard time deciding what he wanted to do with his life. Born in Mount Airy, North Carolina, in 1926, Andy was an only child who took to music at an early age. When he entered the University his goal was to be a minister. After the first year he changed his mind and studied music. He was president of the University Glee Club and graduated with a degree in music.

Jobs were not easy to find in 1949, so Andy applied for and got a job as a high school English teacher. His English students could never have guessed that Andy would achieve fame by badly misusing the English language in his "country style" monologues "What It Was Was Football" and "Romeo and Juliet." His recordings caught the attention of Ed Sullivan and Andy wowed audiences with his appearance on the Ed Sullivan Show.

Andy went on to play both the stage and film roles in the popular No Time for Sergeants. Again, in the part of Will Stockdale, he slaughtered the English language. These parts led to his most popular television series, The Andy Griffith Show, which introduced viewers to the small town of Mayberry and Sheriff Andy Taylor. In a round about way Andy got his wish to be a minister. Every episode, while humorous, dealt with values.

Griffith's career took a downhill slide after he left the Andy Griffith Show in 1968. He had parts in two unsuccessful movies and made pilots for two television series that were turned down. His role as a prosecuting attorney in the television film Fatal Vision caught the attention of NBC executives and Andy was back on top with his popular series Matlock.

The re-runs of the Andy Griffith Show and Matlock have made Andy Griffith one of television's most beloved performers. In semi-retirement he continues to make TV guest appearances and play supporting roles in films.

FACT OR FICTION?

Michael Landon
was the top student
in his high school graduating class.

Michael Landon

Eugene Orowitz (Michael Landon) was born in 1936, in Queens, New York. Always small for his age, Michael grew up in a home where his parents continually fought, and his mother lavished all her attention on his sister while either ignoring or punishing Michael. Despite an IQ that some reported to be as high as 159, Michael was third to the last student in his high school graduating class. He was small, weighing only 126 pounds. He was shy, picked on a lot, and hid his his fear of bullies with jokes and wild escapades.

As a young teen Michael saw the movie Sampson and Delilah, and discovering that strength came from Sampson's long hair, Michael grew his hair long. He soon became the best javelin thrower on the track team and held the record for the longest throw by any high school student at that time. College scholarships were offered, but Michael had to work hard to get his grades high enough to attend college. Once again he had trouble fitting in with his college teammates. His college career ended quickly with an injury to his throwing arm.

Michael got a job in a filling station across from Warner Brothers Studios. An executive there noticed the good looking boy and told him to enroll in the Warners Acting School. This led to small parts in a variety of films until in 1959 Michael won the role of Little Joe Cartwright in the hit TV series Bonanza. The series lasted fourteen years, and Michael played in every episode doing many of his own stunts.

After Bonanza, Michael starred to two other popular series, Little House on the Prairie and Highway to Heaven. At age 54, Michael Landon had had three marriages. His nine children were devastated to learn that their father had inoperable cancer. Within three months of the diagnosis, Michael Landon passed away.

The legacy left by this talented actor is the value of a warm and loving family and compassion for fellow human beings and the trials we all face.

FACT OR FICTION?

Barbara Walters planned a career
as a writer rather than an interviewer
because she spoke with a lisp.

Barbara Walters

Barbara Walters, born in Boston, Massachusetts, in 1931, grew up surrounded by famous people. Her father, Louis Walters, was an agent who represented many stars. He also owned a chain of nightclubs and was a Broadway producer. Famous people were frequent visitors, and Barbara grew up thinking of the rich and famous as "every day folk."

After high school and college Barbara joined the NBC Today Show as a writer. She was comfortable with the job behind the camera since she had a distinct lisp in her speech since childhood. It was not long before her writing showed a depth not before seen, and she was allowed to edit her own reports and interviews. During this time she worked to eliminate the lisp. By 1972, Barbara was on camera with in depth interviews of celebrities and became co-host of the Today Show in 1974, the first woman to hold that job.

Perhaps because of her early contact with celebrities, Barbara was not intimidated by the rich and famous. Her down-to-earth interviews caught the imagination of the public, and with her "never give up" attitude Barbara was able to record interviews with many world leaders who rarely made themselves available to the press. Her "scoop" interviews included Boris Yeltsin, Margaret Thatcher, Indria Gandhi, Fidel Castro, and the Shah of Iran.

In 1974, Barbara became the highest paid journalist in television when she signed a five year contract with NBC for one million dollars a year.

In 1999 Barbara became the host of ABCs popular news show 20/20. She continues to appear on many top-rated news specials.

Barbara Walters used her background, her education, and her ability to relate to people, at the same time overcoming her speech problem, to open the doors for women journalists both in television and print media. She was and is a pioneer in journalism who continues to pave the way for others.

ACTORS AND ACTRESSES

ATHLETES

GOVERNMENT AND LAW

SINGERS & MUSICIANS

TELEVISION ACTORS & PERSONALITIES

Additional Reading

CB = Children's Biography **AB** = Adult Biography

Hank Aaron: Brave in Every Way by P. Hank. Gulliver Books, 2005. CB

Hank Aaron, Home Run King by Jacob Margolies. Watts, 1992. CB

Madeleine Albright by Suzanne Freedman. Watts, 1998. CB

Alan Alda by Joseph Bonderoff. Signet, 1982. AB

Alan Alda by Raymond Strait. St. Martins Press, 1983. AB

Julie Andrews: A Life On Stage and Screen by Robert Windeler. Carol Pub., 1997. AB

Lance Armstrong by D. Armentrout. Rourke, 2004. CB

Lance Armstrong by George Stout. Little Brown, 2003. CB

Lance Armstrong by Sandy Donovan. Lerner Sports, 2005. CB

One More Time: A Memoir by Carol Burnett. Random House, 1986. AB

Discovering Doris Day by Tom Santopietro. Dunne, 2006. AB

Doris Day Her Own Story by Doris Day. Morrow, 1976. AB

Hillary Clinton by Suzanne Levert. Millbrook, 1998. CB

Hillary Clinton: The Inside Story by Judith Warner. Signet 1999. AB

Leonardo DiCaprio by Stacey Stauffer. Chelsea House, 1999. CB

Gloria Estefan: International Singing Star by Shelly Neilson. Abdo , 1993. CB

Ella Fitzgerald by Andrea Pinkney. Jump At The Sun, 2003. CB

Lucky Man by Michael J. Fox. Hyperion, 2002. AB

Michael J. Fox by Jill Wheeler. Abdo, 2001. CB

Michael Fox, Courage for Life by Barbara Kramer. Enslow, 2005.

Get Happy: The Life of Judy Garland by Gerald Clarke. Delta, 2001. AB

Andy Griffith Show by Ken Beck. St. Martins, 2000. AB

The Andy Griffith Story by Terry Collins. Explorer Press, 1995. AB

Tom Hanks: Academy Award Winning Actor by Rosemary Wallner. Abdo & Daughters, 1994. CB

Spirit of Bob Hope by Richard Grudens. Celebrity Profiles, 2001. AB

Michael Landon: Life, Love and Laughter by Harry Flynn. Pomgranate, 1991. AB

Michael Landon: His Triumph and Tragedy by A. Joyce. Z Mass, 1991. AB

Coal Miner's Daughter by Loretta Lynn. Regney, 1976. AB

Sandra Day O'Connor by Christopher Henry. Franklin Watts, 1994. CB

Sandra Day O'Connor by Mary Hill. Children's Press, 2003. CB

Colin Powell by Reggie Filayson. Lerner Publications, 2004. CB

Colin Powell by Mary Hill. Children's Press, 2003. CB

Christopher Reeve: Don't Lose Hope by Sunita Aptd. Bearport, 2006. AB

Condoleezza Rice: Being the Best by Mary Dodson Wade. Millbrook Press, 2003. CB

Jackie Robinson: Baseball's First Black Major Leaguer by Carol Greene. Children's Press, 1990. CB

Stealing Home: The Story of Jackie Robinson by Barry Dementer. Scholastic, 1990. CB

Nolan Ryan by Lois P. Nicholson. Chelsea House, 1996. CB

Elizabeth (Taylor) by Randy Taraborelli. Warner, 2006. AB

Elizabeth: The Life of Elizabeth Taylor by Alexander Walker. Grove Press, 2001. AB

Barbara Walters; TV Superstar by Mary Malone. Enslow, 1990. CB

Barbara Walters, Journalist by Helen Remstein. Chelsea House, 1998. CB

John Wayne, The Man Behind the Myth by Michael Munn. NAL, 2005. AB

John Wayne: American by Randy Roberts. Bison Books, 1998. AB